THE SPOONS IN THE GRASS
ARE THERE TO DIG A MOAT

poems by
AMELIA MARTENS

THE LINDA BRUCKHEIMER SERIES
IN KENTUCKY LITERATURE

SARABANDE BOOKS LOUISVILLE, KY

THE SPOONS
ARE THERE TO

IN THE GRASS DIG A MOAT

Library of Congress Cataloging-in-Publication Data

Martens, Amelia.
[Poems. Selections]
The spoons in the grass are there to dig a moat : prose poems / by Amelia Martens. -- First edition.
pages ; cm
ISBN 978-1-941411-23-0 (softcover : acid-free paper)
I. Title.
PS3613.A77773A6 2016
811'.6--dc23
2015027058

Cover design and interior by Kristen Radtke.
Manufactured in Canada.
This book is printed on acid-free paper.

Sarabande Books is a nonprofit literary organization.

This project is supported in part by an award from the National Endowment for the Arts.

The Kentucky Arts Council, the state arts agency, supports Sarabande Books with
state tax dollars and federal funding from the National Endowment for the Arts.

for Britton

for Thea and Opal

CONTENTS

THE APOLOGY

And the apology I made for you came from a willow tree. From a lemon. From some mud I found in the living room. Our daughter thinks you are a giant. She asks you to lift the house, so she can put her dolls in timeout. There is a crack in the back of my mind and I am filling it up with forget-me-nots and sailor's knots and do nots. There is a place behind my retina where I am fragile. If I see a sun, if I see a squid, if I see something shiny, I should pick it up. I should turn my head. I should stop watching you while you sleep because I am going to wake you up. I am going to wake up. I am sorry and you have gone to buy more mousetraps.

A FIELD

Once upon a time there was a fly. Once upon a time there was an ache shaped like a sunflower, at least to the eye. Once upon a time a field lay down in a patch of gods and got shot through the gut with cotton and wheat. Once upon a time all grass was seagrass and we swam, serrated by the blades of all known light.

WE WILL BE LONG GONE

By the time Earth is pulled into the sun. No, this won't happen while you are asleep. Not tonight. Those are crickets. Yes, they have wings. The sound comes from their legs, like violins. Not violence. Close your eyes please. The sun is on the other side of the world because other people need day. Because we need night. Because that is how your body is made. Yes, your body is magic. Close your eyes please. The sun that went into your eyes, into your skin, into the ground today, will come up tomorrow. Yes, I'm pretty sure there are others. The moon is not the sun. Yes, they might be married. Goodnight.

POSTCARD FROM THE END

The war was beautiful when it started. Men hung from streetlights, their bodies pressed to poles to catch a glimpse of paper rockets. For each device: a hundred thousand dollar bills were dipped in glue and wrapped around a blue balloon. Pop-pop. Then steady hands readied rockets filled to the brim with gunpowder. A short fuse fit just through the pinhole, and women drank beer when they'd finished their shiftwork building similar bombs across the street. Children danced on broken glass of classroom windows. They sang songs about flowers and plagues.

FREE TIME

All around me people are falling on their forks. We drag comet tails through the streets like forgotten capes. We need a bandage. We need an adage, an adverb, a mountain sage. There's a ringing in my eon. Whoever asks to, can come in. Raise your hand. The covers we pull up are made of magazines. Dear *Atlantic*, could you print something that doesn't make me weep? I'm drying here. I want to mail you my heart. The part where you say *ocean*, the part where you say *sure thing*, the part where I turn into sky.

MARATHON

Jesus hears a swarm of bees beneath his porch. His television screen repeats the scene: runners blown off their lightweight frames, bystanders turned curbside amputees. Another urban cloud of smoke, the street littered with more paper. A man says a bomb doesn't have to be big; thousands don't have to die. An explosion of any size is enough. Shrapnel. Concussions. Lost shoes. Within the hour, automatic rifles hang heavy on shoulders in subway tunnels and established checkpoints. The female anchor, in her navy blazer, says there might be surveillance video: a darkskinned man, a backpack left behind. Someone will answer for this, she says. He knows it's only a matter of time until the bees will want to come inside.

PRE-ALICE

Our daughter steps on roly-polies. She lifts black bodies from the sidewalk, and drops them into her green plastic bucket. *How old are my hands? How old is our house?* She says she wants to see what will happen. *Why does grass bleed on my feet? Does it scream?* She carries her bucket with two hands, bends the red garden gate, and steps stone to stone, toward dill and oregano. *Their bodies are good for the vegetables.* We watch from the far side of the parabola; it's not all downhill from here, but it looks that way. Before dinner, we find her in the bathroom as she unloads more bodies from her pocket into the drain. *Who did Anne Frank get to be next?*

ALREADY AT WAR

Jesus grips the wheel. Turns to watch shadows spread like stains across the grass median. Bits of paper and cigarette butts, a haphazard garden plot between two strips of cement. It's been forty minutes and Jesus has driven two miles; he can almost see the freeway. All around him hope is lost, tossed from car windows. Now, the DJ wants everyone to call in, to vote: which video trending on YouTube should be used to announce the war? Jesus closes his eyes and sees the bodies of oarfish, washed up on the beach. An outcome of Japan's nuclear fallout. Fracking. Mythical beasts that foreshadow massive earthquakes. Yesterday, off the coast of Catalina, fishermen found the skeleton of a Volkswagen, filled with finger bones all pointing west.

DEAR BRIAN TURNER

Our daughter thinks you're sad. She saw your picture on the back of *Phantom Noise* and said your eyes look hurt. I described the war in terms that no one can understand. Everything I say will be on the playground tomorrow. She thought your mouth looked okay. She also liked the birds on the cover. *A helicopter is a type of bird, momma.* I did not read her the poem for your unborn daughter. I did not say what I think you are trying to say. I mentioned nothing about shrapnel, white space, or how it is to be inside your self inside the dark. Maybe next time a profile? Something near water, the focus a little less sharp?

SHORELINE

Tonight is gut-shot with fireflies. The whole town is down by the river watching sky get drunk on gunpowder. Every year can be rolled like this piece of paper and slipped into a bottle. *Domestic violence* sounds soft, like pocket lint or game-show laughter. You think that bottle cap is a lucky charm. You think everyone carries an opener. You say *worst-case scenario* and I am standing in the war. I am standing in the water. How far to the barge of fire? How far upstream do I begin? What do my eyes look like from space?

BEDTIME

It doesn't matter that night is pulling up in the driveway. Owlets open their eyes, crescent moon and filament. Seahorses are all dying. In one bedroom, monkeys gather around a blanket and wait for the light to go out. In another, blackout curtains were installed, pre-war, and the mirror shows only cloud below the waist. Elsewhere, someone's daughter just doused herself in gasoline and the missing girls are still missing. In the kitchen, a man and a woman cling to each other, momentarily, while a thunderclap stomps their bungalow and chases the dog from his pillow.

WHEN PEOPLE LOOK TO THE SKY

Angels are falling so fast they are invisible to the human eye. Sometimes they burst on impact and carry away a wedding party. Sometimes they come apart above a school and a mural of ten-year-olds appears on the playground in black ashen outlines. There is an inclination to look directly at the sun; this should be avoided. The cornea is a cradle and can only hold light of the right size. Angels often burn too bright and move like delicate arrows into any open eye. After that, night. The people shift rubble and the city is a garden of headstones worn smooth by blind fools.

IN THE FIRST WORLD

The moon is pink. Husks of cicada and hummingbird corpses litter the sidewalk. Our daughter plots a ceremony at her plastic table. She draws a picture for your grandmother who isn't dead. She whispers thank yous for tiny teddy bears, stolen from your other grandmother's bed. The one who is dead. She counts to seven and tells me I have stolen a letter from the alphabet; I have stolen the eight. Here, the people eat endless appetizers and die from sadness.

IN GOD'S COUNTRY

The Messiah works the drive-thru. His fingers tap a touch screen to call up orders of fries, buckets of diet cola, and sides of cinnamon bites. Static voices fill his ears like an ocean. Each demand is translated as a typed command for the team standing over vats of oil boiling in the back.

By his first smoke break, even the hairnet hangs heavy. Out back at the dumpster, he thinks about how to help. How he might offer napkins, thin as onion skins, and sweep the path clear with his palms as he hands over a grease-stained bag.

His window only opens halfway. But it's enough space for Jesus to look drivers in the eye. Enough time to tell them he knows, they know, we're all heading uphill to die.

.

B-I-N-G-O

Goldilocks's daddy is carried around by his neck. His bib, cross-stitched with "Baby" and a small orange giraffe, is a double-knotted chokehold. Goldilocks drives fast. She zooms through the dining room, past the record player, and crashes into the dishwasher. Once the dog stops barking, she steps from her red roadster and surveys the landscape. *What does debris mean? What does intact mean?* A herd of farm animals freeze as she strolls over and plucks a goat like a guitar string, until he pops off the gray pasture and falls to his death in the heating vent. Over the loudspeaker, the voice of God sings: *There was a farmer, had a dog...*

DON'T MISS OUR MOWER AND TRACTOR SPECTACULAR

Little machines pile up. A watering can splits apart and spreads across the lawn. There's a shelf lined with jars and industrious spiders work in shifts to crochet lids. We fill the basement up like lungs, while our daughter sprinkles lint; she wants to catch blackbirds that punctuate the driveway. We apologize to worms and slip sunflower seeds into fat pockets of earth. We hope for an ocean of golden means, to raise us from this dirt.

DIRECT CONTACT

Our daughter wishes on a star. *Momma, my body is made of stars.*
Your body is made of star parts. I wish on a star. On Mars, the engi-
neers are all eyes, all ears. They wait for the last shoe to drop. For a
comet that once lived near the sun to return from icy hibernation,
for the scientists to read a message of original matter. Why does it
matter if Mars was covered in vast, shallow oceans? The Curiosity
is set down on a red-dust ruffle by ropes and rockets. On Earth,
the engineers sigh and shuffle their cards. Their next mission:
how to seal off airports. First Dallas, then Kennedy.

BAGGAGE

Jesus waves his wand over abdominal muscles buried under a sea of fat. He casts his net of electronic waves over breasts, slides it over thighs, and waits for the beep to increase as he listens to a thousand heart-beaten passengers pull their shoes off and frown.

Yesterday, he worked the x-ray scanner. Sat on a stool, glued to the blue screen, and watched the bones of suitcases, the outline of a grenade never far from his mind. He thought about a gun made of socks, what two hands could do with a bra stripped of its under-wire, how easily books might bludgeon.

By noon they pull Jesus from the line; his eyes and beard are making people uncomfortable. No one mentions his skin, but they think they see him smile sadly each time contraband—a lighter or water bottle—is confiscated.

In the evening, he ushers people to their gates through a tube; they are made to hold their hands above their heads as tiny blasts of air blow away their memories.

IN THE FIRST WORLD

The dialogue is about portfolios. Meaning antibiotics aren't worth our time. Meaning research doesn't jive with the bottom line; dimes are high-wire dancers and some of you are going to die. Pill makers are busy making pills, and pill pushers are busy pushing pills, and pill poppers are busy popping pills. Meanwhile, the bacteria have found chinks in the armor. The moat is dry and the drawbridge is down. In the courtyard, doctors wave prescription pads like white flags as patients build resistance like nobody's business. Just like no body's business.

IN THE LAND OF MILK

Everyone waits for the honey. Mouths are open and tongues dry, even as cream leaks from their lips. Here no lactation can erase visions of thick golden sap dripping from the fuzzy legs of bees. When the mail truck drives through town, people fall to their knees in hope the door might slide back and a soft package, like those bags used to collect blood, will be delivered unto them. In homage, parents name their children Alfalfa, Clover, Orange Blossom, and these children grow like weeds. In school they learn to evaporate. They become obsessed with shelf life and walk home in puffs of white dust. In gym, they load hives of corrugated boxes and then their offering is shipped away, to babies who dream of paper cows filled with powder.

A HUNDRED MILES FROM THE BORDER

Even Jesus knows it takes three Americans to do the work of one immigrant, so he's farmed out the labor.

Now poor boys from Mexico City stand on the assembly line, hot irons in their hands, and brand the face of the Virgin onto grilled cheese sandwiches, mud flaps, and the backs of lace curtains.

Soon the new wing will open up and Jesus will expand his operation; he's slipped St. Peter a little something on the side, insurance against star-chested archangels riding up in a flurry of lights.

Since the installation of the air conditioner, the boys don't mind being paid in Hail Marys and signed notes for salvation. They work mostly by candlelight, branding to the murmurs of Jesus as he works his rosary like an abacus.

MORNING GIRL

All day long you followed me. I sprinkled Cheerios for you, my persistent chicken. In between fists, you spoke a language I would not understand for a thousand years. Even with two birds in my hand. Even if I was my other self. All day long the sun endured and came down to be eaten by the asphalt, across the black span of space to a black span of space. We think we are living here. We think we will live here a little longer. Now you are pulling books from the pile. There are some things you are trying to tell me, some things that can't be burned.

AND THEN THE IDEA OF WEEDS

The idea. The very idea. Out of loneliness. The profoundness of being, and the being, and the being alone, and the being alone knowing, and the being alone knowing that you could create a beginning. And then the beginning. And then the need for an ending. And then the days. And then the figuring out how to order the days so there could be a beginning and an ending. Daybreak. And then the settling back into mythology, but not oblivion. And then a field of gods.

LATE NIGHT COMEDY

We listen to our daughter cry while frogs uncork their throats. An owl in our oak hits each note necessary to pull a white mouse to the sky. If she needs to ask, then I need to tell her why.

Our daughter wants to know if monsters are alive. *Like dinosaurs, were they, but then they died?* I have no proof. No photos or bones. Monsters are alive, somewhere. *But what are monsters?* The unnamed unknown, a problematic point of view. She asks me to lift her, so she can squish a carpenter ant as it crawls up the doorjamb. *We are monsters, momma. And we don't even live under a bridge.*

You want to tell her something like you mean it. Go on. There's an opening coming up to your right. A turnstile, a spinning wheel. Touch it. There are people we don't know; there are so many people we don't know.

COLLECTION

Jesus dumps a jar of buttons on the table. He's looking for monkey eyes, for security, for a way to keep his pants up. He needs something to thread. A way to make sense of the black holes, the dissolving in his sleep. A method of approach against the cold. He separates change, bits of lint, liquor receipts. A wheat penny clicks against a Buffalo nickel and Jesus gets out his solder gun. He needs to melt metal, fashion a backing, make a little unexpected spectacle. Something to reflect the sun, the strain, the string theories fraying his mind.

IN THE DAYS BEFORE THANKSGIVING

Yellow leaves cascade into an intersection on a slow news morning. *Do this.* A kitten crawls into a sewer drain. *In remembrance of me.* A man punches a woman in the face. *Do this in remembrance of me.* A child coos to a baby doll in a plastic stroller. *Do this.* Squirrels chitchat an oak tree and near centerfield, a boy on a mower surveys empty grandstands. *In remembrance.* Husks of mammoth sunflowers stand frozen in our garden, faces bowed and cast east. A tribe of broken bodies. We tried, but our bodies were already broken. Tired, our bodies all broke down. The light turns from red to green, from green to yellow. *Of me.* Leaves are crushed against asphalt.

PLUTO WAS A PLANET

Our daughter claims there's a bone caught in her heart. She can hear it. Beat, beat, beat. The car behind me beeps while I reframe her face in the rearview. How often I don't see what's behind me. After a night of deep freeze, the earth is so solid beneath my feet, I question gravity. We are relative. We are sunlight. She is upset. Zero is her favorite number, but nothing begins there. We stand on an island of frozen food and her hand is a rainbow bruise. There is a paper cut on my heart, in the shape of a heart. She tells me I made her blood. I made, I made, I made.

TUESDAY

By the time Jesus leaves the stadium, every bridge has been
blown up. Cardboard castles burn down in the background. Li-
ons drink from fountains made of seraphim and abandoned cars
make impromptu parking lots. Shadows cut alleyways through
brick and hush streetlights. Somewhere nearby, a man once
dreamed of a bread truck, and was devoured by saber-toothed
data. Sometimes no one says *enough is enough; enough is too far
away*. Sometimes Jesus goes back to work, having forgotten
what he was going to say.

UNION

Every morning our daughter builds a small memorial. She gives us each a flowered plastic plate of plastic cake, so we can remember her when she dies. She cries because her hair isn't fixed right. The day is bright sunlight, but too cold to burn dinner in her playhouse. She wants us to melt the snow. She wants to know more about the chicken in my thigh, the blood in the toilet bowl. *What color are my insides? Of my egg? Am I yellow?* She cries because federal employees can't receive presents, then works for hours with a small chisel and pick. During lunch she announces apologies and future plots. She wants to take my heart out and sweep every room.

FORECAST

He has heard of an island within a lake, within an island, within an ocean. He wakes up to gray morning coming on outside. There is no coffee. Across the alley, his neighbor's dog complains. Jesus listens to what it means to be chained. He pours orange juice and turns on the news. Everyone is going to die. He knows the sun is up, but clouds keep shadows tucked away. With California in his mouth, he watches the weather reporter wave her arms from west to east, as if this explains everything. The warming waters of the Pacific have twisted Tornado Alley. Again, he thinks of that island within the lake, within the island, within the ocean. He knows this is where the locusts beat their gossamer wings, their threads heating the jet stream. This is where the frogs begin.

THE PRINCE OF PEACE IS HERDING SHEEP

No, he's in west Texas collecting cattle. One by one, he touches their heads and they drop dead. A summer of drought and little tolerance for the hand of God. They fall lightly in the dust as Jesus rides his donkey across creosote flats. Fifteen thousand beasts in three days; the cows cluster around tiny pools, smothering each other with overheated hearts. Too slow to move apart. Jesus wipes his brow and surveys the carnage. Just enough meat on those bones to feed the ghosts rising like smoke from the Horn of Africa. Two million children evaporate, as college football fans rush parking lots for the first tailgate of the season.

INEXPLICABLE UNIVERSE

Our daughter is allergic to blue. You ask the doctor to show us the bird's-eye view, the balloon, a photo taken from space. A cold satellite rotates as our omniscient eyeball. Invisible stars live inside her heart. Soon all of my tattoos will fade beneath the ocean of age. Her still-small fingers reach, even in sleep, for my belly button. Our herniated connection. She is our ether and we are distant moons, come together in extended orbit.

LOCALIZED EXTINCTION

They tell me *turn here* and I look out across the pierced ocean. A pier. A splinter. A path of rafters; spaces between boards large enough to swallow our daughter's foot. Timber taken from a fog-blanket up north, where no one would miss another dismantled shipwreck. The timbre of the ocean like a heartbeat, like salt-soaked axe wounds and scars of metal lashings. Starfish sucking sap, now dying by the thousands. O sea canaries! Tell me I am *here*, when I am not.

IN THE COUNTRY OF NEUTRALITY

The asylum seekers have been banned from public pools. Banned from wearing bathing suits. Banned from being nude. Pretty soon they'll be banned from bus stops; only certain people can be allowed to go up and down all through the town. The good news: IKEA is sponsoring recycled housing for refugees and the furniture is quite stylish. Bold prints hide the dirt, and there's a single-peg coat rack, for that one extra shirt.

WEDNESDAY

By the time Jesus leaves the bar, the sun is already in position.
High noon: a molten tangle of flare encased in a wire basket, a
mass of snapdragon tongues. Who wants that responsibility, that
smoke in their lungs? Jesus fumbles for his keys, considers driving
straight into the ocean licking the end of the street. Past the taco
stand, the inflatable mammals, and over the pile of tired novels.
Why not let his car sink in salt? The engine's already rusted out
and Jesus can't do a damn thing with the moon.

COMING FORTH TO CARRY US

On the brown bathroom rug, our daughter. *What am I doing? I'm dying. You close your eyes when you're dying.* The family of plastic ducks float, little boats sculpted into their backs. Blue. Yellow. Green. All colors make all things. *Close your eyes, momma. Just close your eyes. You are dying.* Goodbye dry skin, dry tub, dry rug. The water level's rising. *Come, dog. Close your eyes. Be dying.*

ROUTINE

Floating on his back in a cow pond, the Prince of Peace practices his out-of-body experience. First, his eyes close and the water climbs his crow's-feet, up dry riverbeds, until it pools over his eyelids. Only his nose breaks the surface. Jesus does not breathe, but tiny ripples echo off his body, pushed to shore by his heartbeat. Then, even this stops. His nose disappears and the surface is back to reflecting sky, which has broken into a sunset, like heaven shifting into fall. Red, orange, purple. The cows turn west; flies hum their ears. Overhead, Jesus looks down, watches two fireflies blink their neon song and counts back from ten. He raises his own body from the mud, wipes the world from his eyes, and makes his way across the field.

WE ASK FOR FIVE MINUTES

We are simple people. The small pleasures: hot water, silence, waking up on our own. Nothing is missed until it evaporates. Our skin is lifting off even as we sink in bracelets of tiny anchors. The only t-shirt you wear has a hole in the back. Our daughter wonders who stabbed you. Who rolled us through fields of plastic cutlery and sippy cups? Who surrounded our bed with rubber ducks and pressed the thermometer too hard, too often, to our foreheads? At the end of the day, the peach always falls into the ocean and we've come too late to have anything to say.

THE ROBIN PULLS A THREAD

And Jesus plucks his beard. He sits on a park bench watching coal barge down the Ohio as this bird unspools his shirt. *Made in Bangladesh. Made in Vietnam. Made in Afghanistan. Pakistan. Cambodia.* The red thread extends as this robin holds it tender in her beak. The light orange of her chest reminds him of a garment fire. How flames licked the windows and sparred with hangers piled against chained exit doors. The picture in the paper showed a building folded into black ash. Burned patterns of bones that never spoke English. How alluring the thorn crown must have looked. The perfect nest. In the cold spring air, Jesus pulls off the rest of his shirt. His chest is dyed a pale red. *Made in China.* Even the robin seems shocked at the price.

ALMOST BIBLICAL

Before the garden, two girls played together on a blue rug. One wore monkey pajamas and had wild, tumbleweed hair. The smaller girl wore monsters and a single ponytail, like a whale spout, out the top of her head. First, they opened the box. First, everything had to be taken out. First, the continents were one and then they were broken. In the beginning, the snake was whole. Then his body segmented, and the two girls moved on, wanting to see what made him.

HISTORICAL ACCURACY

Two Lincolns duel sunlight on the sidewalk. If this is all in my mind, what is this pain in my chest? You think every river can manage a bridge. You think there is a way across this expanse of cloud-cover come down. Your concept is all horizon. Mine is a card catalogue of sound. It's only an idea: the turnstile. Last night, I put you on the roof again and let my fault line shine clear through. I made you into the Wild West: the toothpick and tumbleweed, dust and glare. After they'd made it to the ocean, some people turned around.

PINK PIGS AND ORANGE HORSES

You think you are the lost princess, but your hair isn't long enough. Someone has been riding your giraffe. Every morning, the rooster raises the sun from his throat. A wolf is trapped in your bathroom; he huffs and puffs against the tub. Someone has been rifling though your toy box. The spoons in the grass are there to dig a moat. There is no explanation about the cookies. Someone has been wearing your clothes and they fit just right. In the event of a water landing, nothing you own will turn into a boat.

DUST

Jesus folds the newspaper in half. Every day a mother locks her daughter in the closet. Every day a breathing newborn is slipped into a trash bag and buried in the backyard. Every day a hunter finds a toddler's body in the woods, just as the sun crawls over blue mountains. Every day a man shoots his estranged wife in the back of her head: in a grocery store, in a mall parking lot, in her bedroom. Every day the prayers of a billion people don't get airplay. Every day the ink dries. He orders another drink. Across the street, smoke rises from the ammunition plant. He remembers his father's words: all is dust. Even a sugar factory can turn to flame.

POSTCARD FROM THE END 2.0

We wait for our turn to explode. There is a line; tickets are punched and dropped in a glass box by a man in a straw hat. Someone cranks a phonograph and Bob Dylan carries the bones of Woody Guthrie up a dirt road. Bicycles are abandoned in the grass. Then a velvet rope is lifted and ushers brush the air with wide palms. The parade circles a farmhouse; canned laughter works its way through the plumbing. In the barn, cows mock the moon. People watch the news in rooms filled with hydrogen balloons, where matches are passed out like cigarettes.

NEWTOWN

Like a cement statue, Jesus sits amidst a funnel cloud of flipped-over plastic chairs. All the desks show signs of stress. Names remain written on whiteboards and stars still mark good behavior. The furnace kicks on. Papers trestle the dead teacher's desk on their way to the floor. There is nothing he can do. In the coming days, out-of-state cleaning crews will descend like crows to lift only the lightest stains. Where they fail, the carpet must be cut away. The town whispers his father's name in hyphenated damn its, while on his head thorns turn like screws.

DISNEY DAUGHTER DEAD, 2013

Sleeping Beauty is surrounded by thorn bushes. She's sleeping in the same forest as Snow White. The dwarfs can't handle grief. Don't know what to do with the swell that rises in their wishing wells. They lift pickaxes and chip away at the mine's sparkly ceiling. Death and diamonds are all they believe in. They don't whistle while they work.

In the garden, Cinderella is a mound by the pumpkin patch. Mice crisscross her chest in patterns, fork marks on piecrust. She was buried in her glass slippers. Buried in her best dress. Buried outside the castle walls, among the skeletons of orange trees. From the doorway, she watched her daddy draw at his desk. She knew who made the universe, the apple, and the blood in her fingertips.

THE SECRET LIVES OF COWS

They do not type letters to Farmer Brown. They do not jump over the moon. They are not sold to buy magic beans. They do not kick lanterns and ignite Chicago. All night long they breathe cold air, their nostrils damp thimbles. They tamp earth down to the dust it has been for millennia. All night long they nurse an ache, a tender machine in the underbelly, which never goes dormant. Not even during the flood, when they raise their heads from second-floor porches and watch pastures drift away.

MIDDLE AMERICA

In one hand Jesus holds a seed: a brain, already mapped and waiting for a cloudburst. He can feel the most delicate trigger, the fingers of farmers as they steer wheels of two-ton machines and turn soil into something else. A landscape scraped of grass once blew away for an entire decade, and Jesus knows it could happen again. He closes his palm around the seed, plants his hands in his overall pockets, and follows the barbed wire, marked every thousand yards by a sign for chemically resistant corn. He hears his father's thunderclap laugh. Flocks of sheep watch the sunset. All is sacred; what better life can be designed?

BIRTH DAY

Two girls with hummingbird hearts lay across my chest, across my stomach, across my legs. They crisscross their limbs and keep me like gravity. They are my multiverse, and momentarily, I am the maker, not the sun. Their daddy might be the sun. Soon the sun will come in the window and the birds of my heart will stir and nuzzle and begin to peck each other, their eyes still closed. Their hands move through dreams to map my face, open. They are oceans come into being. They blink and set my watch.

HEARTWOOD

As he walks through the cemetery, the Prince of Peace grazes the tips of potted Christmas trees. Wrapped in purple cellophane or dotted with gold bows. Jesus knows no one is coming back. Tomorrow is always Epiphany. The trees have been abandoned to the grace of gravestones. Monday morning, the maintenance crew will gather a miniature pine forest in the back of their pick-up truck. Between the cemetery and the freeway, a line of pine grows thick with leftover holiday cheer. At the center of each tree, a cross grows, which no one but the saw-man will ever see.

IN THE FIRST WORLD

Parents peel film from pages of plastic. Delicate in their hands, the plastic bows; they apply it evenly to each window. This coating can't stop a bullet, but it will keep the window from breaking into shards of spiderweb, a hole to let a hand in. It was not enough to lock the front door. The parents realize glass as a primary weakness. They let go fears of a classroom fire, gas leaks, carbon monoxide, and atomic bombs. At last their terror has found a focus. They realize the error; they want nothing to do with what may shatter.

PEN PAL

Jesus considers answering some mail. He sorts the stack from yesterday into three piles: picture requests, pleas for healing, and questions of biblical proportion. To prevent identity theft, he carries heap one over to the shredder and crisscross cuts it to oblivion. Jesus reads through the mountain of people who would like their sight restored, their backbones straightened, the bottle removed. He tears these pages into confetti and brews a troubled tea. Last, Jesus jots psalm numbers like barcodes across the remaining envelopes and writes: *Not @ this address.*

THEY SHOOT PEOPLE, DON'T THEY?

Much of the world is current on their hunger strike. I can't tell our daughters everything will be all right. They are less afraid of the dark than of the light. Our keelboat has run aground. Yesterday, another man opened a door in someone's chest. You think we are coming around. You think we are blessed. Homeward bound. What is there to confess? The parts per million. The humming-bird needles. The losses so fine we shed them with our skin.

MAGICICADA

Icarus confetti. Skeins of flight fallen. Right wings. Left wings. A thousand vacancies. An invasion of time travelers shed their husks on the lawn and we track them in like grass. Miniature black and velvet mummies, their tymbal bellies alarm the trees. We are waiting for the reburial. The tunnel-dig to turn around. We rock our envy on porch swings, jealous of those who leave their bodies. We would live for years underground, if only we could learn how.

ACKNOWLEDGMENTS

Grateful acknowledgment is made to the editors and readers of the following journals where these poems originally appeared in various forms:

The Chattahoochee Review: "In the Land of Milk," "A Hundred Miles from the Border"
The Hampden-Sydney Poetry Review: "Pre-Alice," "A Field"
Iron Horse Literary Review: "Baggage"
pacificREVIEW: "Tuesday," "Forecast"
Southern Humanities Review: "The Apology," "Postcard from The End"
Squalorly: "Collection," "Pink Pigs and Orange Horses"
South Dakota Review: "We Will Be Long Gone," "Free Time," "Already at War"

Thank you Britton, for our life. Thank you Canyon and Rebecca, forever. Mom and Dad, words and power. Rosie and Fritz, Millie and Ben. Shurley family, for bringing me in. Valdes family. Julie, forever. Geoff. T-Rex. Finola and Caydence. Lucy, for the life raft. Thank you to the mommas, you are strong beyond words. Thank you Deals, Worley-Perrys, Abdons, Coopers, and Leacocks. Wallace family, daily dharma. Romayne and Bob. Michael Crouse of BrokenStone Press. Diane Goettel and Kit Frick of Black Lawrence Press. Bricolage Art Collective. Thank you Richard Cecil,

Maurice Manning, Nin Andrews, Max Garland, Lynnell Edwards, Catherine Bowman, and Nathaniel Perry. Mason Tudor and the WKCTC family. I am grateful to Linda Bruckheimer, to Sarah Gorham and to the Sarabande team for their careful raising up of these poems. This book was encouraged by *The Rose Metal Press Field Guide to Prose Poetry: Contemporary Poets in Discussion and Practice*, edited by Gary L. McDowell and F. Daniel Rzicznek. I appreciate Barry Spacks, Indiana University's MFA program, the Kentucky Women Writers Conference, and support from the Kentucky Arts Council. Thea and Opal, I will always be in awe of you.

AMELIA MARTENS received an MFA in Creative Writing from Indiana University. She lives in Paducah and teaches as an adjunct instructor at West Kentucky Community & Technical College where she helps edit *Exit 7*. She received an Emerging Artist Award from the Kentucky Arts Council in 2010. Her poems have appeared in *Crab Creek Review*, *Whiskey Island*, *Willow Springs*, and elsewhere. She is the author of three chapbooks: *Purgatory*, which won the Fall 2010 Black River Chapbook competition (Black Lawrence Press, 2012), *Clatter* (Floating Wolf Quarterly, 2013), and *A Series of Faults* (Finishing Line Press, 2014). She is married to the poet Britton Shurley; they have two smart, beautiful, brave daughters and a ridiculous dog.

Sarabande Books is a nonprofit literary press located in Louisville, KY, and Brooklyn, NY. Founded in 1994 to champion poetry, short fiction, and essay, we are committed to creating lasting editions that honor exceptional writing. For more information, please visit sarabandebooks.org.